FIND IT FAST

6TH
EDITION

A wonderful book . . . highly recommended.
—Library Journal

A valuable reference work for anyone digging for information.
—Journalism Quarterly

For serious researchers, this book is a gold mine.
—Choice